ABUNDANT LIFE

ABUNDANT LIFE

Maxine Lantz

WestBow
PRESS
A DIVISION OF THOMAS NELSON

WestBow Press books may be ordered through booksellers or by contacting:

WestBow Press
A Division of Thomas Nelson
1663 Liberty Drive
Bloomington, IN 47403
www.westbowpress.com
1-(866) 928-1240

Because of the dynamic nature of the Internet, any web addresses or links contained in this book may have changed since publication and may no longer be valid. The views expressed in this work are solely those of the author and do not necessarily reflect the views of the publisher, and the publisher hereby disclaims any responsibility for them.

Certain stock imagery © Thinkstock.
Any people depicted in stock imagery provided by Thinkstock are models, and such images are being used for illustrative purposes only.

ISBN: 978-1-4497-5598-0 (e)
ISBN: 978-1-4497-5597-3 (sc)

Library of Congress Control Number: 2012910516

Printed in the United States of America

WestBow Press rev. date: 9/21/2012

AUTHOR'S FOREWORD

I have called this booklet of poetry "Abundant Life" because that is what I have been given, not filled with what the world views as abundance, but full of the love, peace, mercy and grace of my Lord. I hope that these poems will give you some insight into what I believe is the true character of God and his son, Jesus Christ. I thank God for saving me, and I look forward to spending eternity with God and Jesus Christ.

I pray that these poems will edify the reader, and that those who know Christ as Saviour will be encouraged to continue their walk with him. For the reader that does not yet know Christ in this personal way, I pray that these words will lead you to the point in your life where you will accept Christ as your personal Saviour.

I would also like to take this opportunity to thank the keepers of my words. Each poem I write gets sent to my sister (Lynda Taylor), my husband Jim, my pastor and his wife (John & Cheryl Scorgie, who are also dear friends), and to another two friends (Carrol Ross and Joyce Lindsay). They are my biggest supporters, and I thank them for their love, loyalty and faithfulness.

Thank-you,
Maxine Lantz

Other Books By This Author:

Rhyming Revelation
Love On The Wing
Flights Of Fancy
Covenant Of Care
Basking In The Son-Shine

CONTENTS

BLESSINGS FOR BABY

If I had the power to make wishes come true,
Then these are the blessings I'd ask God for you.
The first is that your life would be filled up with love-
The love of your family and of God up above.
The next, for creation, a respect and concern
Through all that you'll see and all that you'll learn.
I pray that throughout life, you will take a chance
And not stay in your "safe" place so that you will enhance
The world that surrounds you. And the people you meet
Will know that you love them as your actions they see.
I pray that you'll have a real servant's heart
That you'll use to help others as God's love you impart.
I also would pray that you never would let
Circumstance, creed or colour ever make you forget
That all people are made in God's image and so
To each person you meet, His great love you must show.
Another great blessing that I'd wish for you now
Is that, in any moment, you'll always know how
To comfort, encourage and make people feel
The love that you show them is God's love and real.
And then I would wish that you'll have many friends
Who love you and on whom you can always depend.
I pray that, through life's dance, as each new day falls,
That sometimes you'll jig and sometimes you'll waltz.
No matter the tempo, I pray that you'll know
You're held firm in God's hand, as onward you go.
And last, but not least, I pray that you'll see
Your need of the Savior and thus bow your knee.
I pray that this moment will come early in life
And, in times of trouble and in times of strife,
In times of sorrow and in all your good times,
God's peace, grace and mercy you can always find.
These are the blessings that I'd wish for you
If I only had power to make wishes come true.

FOOTPRINTS IN TIME

The scientist looked down and saw
A footprint in the stone.
A single piece of history
That could never be undone.
The person who had left the print
Was nowhere to be found,
And yet the evidence was there
That he walked upon that ground.
I, too, am walking on this earth.
In future times, would they
Be able to discern that I
Had walked in Jesus' way?
Would there be trails to other folk
They could trace from end to start?
Would my spiritual footprints
Have left marks on people's hearts?
Could they tell I tried to show God's love,
Maybe said a few kind words?
Would the evidence they saw right there
Show I followed Christ, the Lord?
So, dear Lord, as I walk each day,
As I lay down a new path,
I pray that you will guide my steps
So my legacy will last -
A legacy of love I've shown
Because I first was loved by you,
A legacy of words that helped
Lead the lost to your love true.
When my soul wings home to heaven,
And you view my trodden path,
I pray I'll hear you say, "Well done.
Your legacy will last."

FREEDOM IS NOT FREE

Through many wars and conflicts,
The truth is always seen
That, no matter what the cause is,
One's freedom is not free.

Men die for higher causes,
And fight for what is right.
Their love for all their brothers
Is what made them join the fight.

And still, like Christ's example,
Lives are yielded up in war
So that others' lives are bettered,
And evil wins no more.

But man cannot release the soul
From abysmal captivity,
As Christ did for world's fallen man.
Christ can grant soul's liberty.

That freedom does not cost at all,
For the blood price has been paid.
Salvation exchanged for sin's stain
When, on Christ, all sin was laid.

And, like the modern soldier,
Whose life was sacrificed,
Christ now has won the battle;
He paid the ultimate price.

So, whether on a battle field,
Or on the cross at Calvary,
We have to know the price was paid,
And our freedom was not free.

I KNOW I'LL NEVER UNDERSTAND

*Come now, let us reason together," says the
LORD. "Though your sins are like scarlet,
they shall be as white as snow; though they are
red as crimson, they shall be like wool.*

Isaiah 1:18 NIV

I know I'll never understand,
And know I'll never see
How a king can give up heaven's joys
To save a wretch like me.
I only know that, for all time,
My soul will fill with praise
For that great sacrifice of love
That saved me by God's grace.

I know I'll never understand
How so much love would give
A chance for this poor sinner,
In eternity, to live.
I only know that, while I live,
I'll tell of God's great love-
He sent his holy precious Son
To die, His love to prove.

I know I'll never understand
Why a king would come to earth
To give this sin-stained heart of mine
A new-found sense of worth.
I only know my heart's release
From Satan's evil plans.
And now I know, with God beside,
I can forever stand.

I know I'll never understand
How that precious red blood flow
Could change my sins like crimson
To new life, white as snow.
**I only know that with each drop
Of Jesus Christ's red blood,
My soul was washed with life anew-
A truly cleansing flood.**

I know I'll never understand;
No reason can I give
Why a king would die on Calv'ry's cross
So that my soul could live.
**I only know it was my sin
That held Christ to that cross,
And yet he yielded up His life
So my soul would not be lost.**

I LOVE YOU

I love you, my love, for your love of the Lord
As you strive His commands to obey.
I love how you show the love of our God
To the people you meet on life's way.

I love how we talk of the Lord and our faith,
How He's changed and improved both our lives.
I love how we share the great truth that we have
That our God is all present, all wise.

I love that you love me, and let me love you.
I believed you would never appear.
I love that you're here now, with arms open wide,
To share laughter, and wipe away tears.

I love how you know just the right thing to say
To encourage, to build up, and care.
I love you because Christ has planned this for us,
And I love the good man that you are.

I love how your laughter can brighten my life
And brings light to the darkest of days.
I've loved you, and love you, and will always love
'Til the good Lord determines our days.

IF WE SIN

My dear children, I write this to you so that you will not sin. But if anybody does sin, we have one who speaks to the Father in our defense—Jesus Christ, the Righteous One.

1 John 2:1 NIV

My dearest children, hear me now,
And do not sin at all.
But if you sin, then you must know,
On Jesus' name to call.
He's sitting at the Father's side
To intercede for you
For He is righteous, Jesus Christ,
And pure and holy too.
Just bring to Him repentant hearts
That know His loving care.
He will forgive your sins in whole,
For He is just and fair.
He sits communing with our God,
In fellowship divine,
The Father, Son and Holy Ghost,
For your sake and for mine.
Our Advocate before the throne
Will intercede and show
That we are all His children
And His favor we will know.
What awesome privilege we have
To have our Counselor near!
With true repentant hearts, we know
Our prayers He always hears.
We wait with great expectancy
On what He will reveal;
His answer will be giv'n in love
To teach us or to heal,
To reconcile us to God
So that we are restored
And stay along God's narrow way
For now and evermore.

IF YOU HOLD TO MY TEACHING

To the Jews who had believed him, Jesus said, "If you hold to my teaching, you are really my disciples. Then you will know the truth, and the truth will set you free.

John 8:31-32 NIV

"If you hold to my teaching,
My true disciples you'll be.
And the truth you'll discover
Will then set you free."
My Lord said these words
To the Jews who believed,
And had called on His name.
A new life they received-
A life of His power,
One of sins washed away!
They followed His teachings
As they walked through each day.

I, too, like those Jews,
Have called on His name
And the great power received
Is today just the same.
My sins have been washed,
And of them there's no trace
For my King won't remember
My previous place.
He's gracious and loving
And to those who believe
He's promised forever
That He'll never leave.

What comfort, what peace,
And what joy that bestows!
For whatever the circumstance,
My dear Jesus knows.
He'll hold me when tears fall;
We'll dance when life's great.
What a truly magnificent,
Glorious state!
He'll lead me and guide me
Along each day's path
And I know that forever
His great love will last.

IF YOUR BROTHER SINS AGAINST YOU

"If your brother sins against you, go and show him his fault, just between the two of you. If he listens to you, you have won your brother over."

Matthew 18:15 NIV

If your brother sins against you,
Go and tell him of his wrong.
Do it after praying to God
And do not bring someone along.
Tell him how the sin affects you;
Tell him how you wish it changed.
Tell him what the Word says of it.
Do it all in Jesus' name.
If your brother listens to you,
Then your brother you have won.
Give the praise and glory to God,
And to Jesus Christ, his son.
But if your brother does not listen,
Then bring two or three along;
They will be the faithful witness
To what is said and what is done.
But again if he won't listen,
Then the church is where you'll go.
And the church will bring it to him,
As God's love to him they show.
But if he won't even listen
To the church, the Scriptures say
Treat him as a tax collector
Or a pagan. But still pray
That the Holy Spirit's working
In his heart will make it sore,
And he'll repent of the wrong way
And the fellowship restore.
And if this happens to you
Then rejoice at what was gained,
For the lost has been restored now.
Give Christ Jesus all the praise!

JESUS IS JUST LIKE ME

Jesus is just like me
For we're alike in many ways.
And he will always be my friend
Throughout my earthly days.
Fully human, although divine,
He lived his life on earth –
That thought brings me much comfort
And gives my own life worth.
The trials and temptations
That come into my life
Are naught compared to Satan's tries
To cause my Jesus strife.
We both have suffered in our lives,
Although my scars are small
And do not near compare to what
Christ did to save us all.
He showed much indignation
When circumstance decreed
I hope that I can do the same
When faced with evil deeds.
And Christ showed great compassion
To those he met each day.
I hope that I can do the same
To the folks along the way.
He never missed a chance to tell
Of God's unfailing love.
I hope that I can do that too,
With help from up above.
But the biggest difference in our lives,
And on this my hopes I pin,
Is that I was born a sinner,
But my Jesus knew no sin.
He knew no sin, yet took the sins
Of all mankind and bore
The cruel torture on the cross,
And opened heaven's door.

For when His blood ran down the cross
From hands, from feet and side
I then could bring my repentant heart
And in his love abide.
I know that I'm a child of God,
A joint heir with Christ, His Son.
And when I slip this poor flawed earth,
And life down here is done
Then I will live forever more,
And fill the skies with praise
That Jesus is just like me
For we're alike in many ways.

JUST

They say that you were just a man,
A teacher, good and wise.
But I know truth and won't believe
The Temptor's greatest lies.

And yet, when thinking over that,
I think I must agree
The word "just" does apply to you,
In all that it could mean.

You're "just" a man that healed the lame,
And caused the blind to see,
And "just" a man who walked on water
On the Sea of Galilee.

You're "just" a man whom demons knew
And feared for who you are,
And "just" a man that tamed the wind
And could read each person's heart.

You're "just" a man who raised the dead,
And turned water into wine.
How could they say you're "just" a man
With these miracles divine?

And "just" is what your actions were
When they used your house for gain.
You drove them out with corded rope
And removed your temple's stain.

But "just" was not your final end
When you hung upon the tree.
You took my place on that cruel cross
And you paid my penalty.

So, "just" my life I yield to you,
All I was, am and will be.
I know that I cannot repay
Your sacrifice for me.

And, "just" because you died for me
But rose victorious from the grave,
My soul will know eternity
For this sinner now is saved.

LOVE REPEATED

Step by step, you walked the road
To Calv'ry's lonely hill.
You could have saved yourself, Lord,
But you fulfilled the Father's will.

Drop by drop, the blood flowed free
From hand, from feet, from side.
You heard the jeers and heard them all
Your holy name deride.

Day by day, I ask you, Lord,
Please help me truly see
And humbly add my gratitude
For the day you died for me.

MEMORY LOSS

She started to forget some things
That she had known for years,
Like where she put the car keys.
She thought it kind of queer.
She always had been able
To remember names and dates,
But now she could not recollect
What, hours ago, she ate.

Her children all were worried,
And tried to help her cope
With little games they tried to play
To try and give her hope.
She opened up the albums
With faces loved and known,
And yet she could not quite recall
The faces she was shown.

And then her memory left her,
But Jesus held His place.
He stayed right there beside her
As she sang "Amazing Grace".
The words that praised her Jesus
From her mind did not depart,
For her yielding to Him early
Had left a mark upon her heart.

She sang words to "The Lighthouse" ,
"Blessed Assurance", and "Wonderful Peace".
"The Old Rugged Cross" was a favorite.
When she praised God, the words never ceased.
And the day that her soul flew to heaven,
Her memory of what Christ had done
Was as clear as the day, when a young girl,
She had yielded her life to God's Son.

MY HOPE IS IN YOU

To you, O Lord, I lift up my soul;
in you I trust, O my God.

Psalm 25:1 NIV

To you, O My Lord,
I do lift up my soul
In my Savior alone
Is my trust placed whole.
Do not let my enemies
Have triumph o'er me
Let all of my foes
Your omnipotence see.

My hope is in you.
I won't ever see shame.
On those who are treacherous,
You will place blame.
Instruct me in your narrow way,
O My Lord,
And teach me your paths
In the light of your word.

Teach me and guide me
Every day in your truth,
For you are my God
And salvation's in you.
My hope is in you, and
Throughout the day long
Your praises will ever
Be heard in my song.

Remember, O Lord,
Your great mercy and love
For that is the way
That you demonstrate love.
Your mercy and love
Are before time began;
I'll tell of your great love
Whenever I can.

Please never remember
All the sins of my youth
For I walk in your way now
And hold to your truth.
My ways, so rebellious,
I ask you forget.
For that was my way
Before you and I met.

But remember me, Lord,
In accord with your love,
I will wait with great joy
To our meeting above.
For you are good, O My Lord,
And I do understand
That in your great love for me
You do have a plan.

You instruct sinners
In your way, and you show
You holy uprightness
And then they can know
All the burdens that lift
From a repentant heart
And a journey with you
They are able to start.

You guide the humble
In all things that are pure
As they walk down your path,
Salvation is sure.
All the ways of the Lord
Are loving and true
Just call on his name
And he will come through.

And those who hold
To the covenant's demands
Will rest, so secure,
In the palm of God's hand.
Though my sin be so large,
Please forget it, my Lord,
For the sake of your name,
As it says in your Word.

Who then is this God
Whom wise men should fear?
God's plan of salvation
Will be made ever clear.
He'll instruct and He'll guide
In God's chosen way
In prosperity, each day
This wise man will stay.

To those men who fear him,
His love will be shown.
He will, without doubt,
Make his covenant known.
My eyes will ever be
On the Lord, for he cares,
And will release my feet
From my enemies' snares.

Turn to me, and bestow
On me mercy and grace
For I'm alone and afflicted,
And I seek your face.
My troubles are multiplied,
Twenty times o'er,
My heart's full of anguish:
I hurt to the core.

Look upon my affliction
And please take away
My sins and distress
As I walk through each day.
My enemies increase
And how fiercely they hate!
I need you, O My Lord,
My existence to save.

I need you, O My Lord,
To rescue my life
For you are my refuge
And in you I hide.
Integrity and uprightness
Protect me days through
And forever, O My Lord,
My hope is in you.

MY LIFE IS A PARABLE

My life is a parable
With meaning unknown
My whole dependence
Is on God's grace-filled throne.

My past has some import;
My present does too.
My future is hidden,
But I know what God'll do.

He'll take all the minutes
Of inconsequence
And add His great mercy,
And they will make sense.

I believe I'm inadequate,
And yet He commands
That I show to all people
His love when I can.

So, with God right beside me,
I'll go through each day
Just walking in faith
On God's one narrow way.

Believing that one day,
When my earthly life ends,
I'll know what the parable
Means, and I'll sense

That my God knew the finish,
And He held my life's plan,
In His omnipotent fingers
As only God can.

MY PRAYER FOR ALL MY DAYS

Help me, Lord, to walk your way.
Guide my steps, O Lord, I pray.
Guard my tongue in all I say.
Help me all your words obey.

Show me, Lord, your children dear.
May my motives be quite clear.
Draw me close and keep me near,
You'll walk with me; I will not fear.

I'll tell the world all that you've done,
That you are God's beloved Son.
On Calv'ry's cross you bled and hung.
Your death ensured our souls were won.

My tongue will utter words of praise
To thank you for your loving grace.
I long to see you face-to-face
When my soul soars up from this place.

MY SALVATION AND MY HONOR

*"My salvation and my honor depend on God;
he is my mighty rock, my refuge."*

Psalm 62:7 NIV

My salvation and my honor
Depend upon my God.
He is my mighty refuge;
He is my steadfast rock.

There is no earthly power
That stands against my King.
No matter circumstance or time,
His praises I will sing.

I need his strength from day to day
For I'm weak and cannot stand
Without the comforting touch of
My Savior's loving hand.

He gives me access to his throne
And bids me enter there
To bring him my petitions
And place them in his care.

In love, my God will listen
And always do what's best.
My knowledge of his mercy
Will give me peace and rest.

And for my time on earth now
As on this earth I trod,
I'll say, "Salvation and my honor
Depend upon my God."

MY SHEPHERD

The Lord is my Shepherd
I'm His and He's mine.
I shall not want
He will ever provide.

He makes me lie down
He enforces my rest.
In pastures of green
He gives me the best.

He leadeth me by
My Shepherd is near.
The waters so still
I have nothing to fear.

He restoreth my soul
None but He this can do.
He leadeth me
He knows the way true.

In righteousness path
I must trust and obey.
For His name's sake
In His power I will stay.

Yea, though I walk
This is one walk I'll see.
Through the valley of death
From all fear I'll be free.

No evil I'll fear
When The Shepherd is by.
For Thou art with me
In your love I'll abide.

Thy rod and thy staff
All resources are thine.
They comfort me
I'm assured I'll be fine.

Thou preparest a table
You supply all I need.
In my enemies' presence
You are mighty indeed!

Thou anointest my head,
By my Shepherd I'm blessed.
My head with thine oil,
You give me your best.

My cup runneth over
Such a gracious supply.
Surely goodness and mercy
All gifts from on high.

Shall follow me
I know this to be true.
All the days of my life
Their end known by you.

And I shall dwell
This my hope here on earth.
In the house of the Lord
A mansion, great worth.

Forever and ever
Where joy will not end.
For the Lord is my Shepherd
He's my Savior and Friend.

MY STRENGTH IS IN THE SOVEREIGN LORD

The Sovereign LORD is my strength; he makes my feet
like the feet of a deer, he enables me to go on the heights.

Habakkuk 3:19 NIV

My strength is in the Sovereign LORD;
He makes my feet like the deer,
And even on the highest heights,
I have no reason to fear.
The deer can jump from crag to crag,
And they never seem to miss.
With God, I leap from trial to trial
And don't fear the deep abyss.
The deer, when faced with span too wide,
Will stop and turn away.
When I am faced with greater trials,
In the will of God I stay.
His holy hand will guide and lead
Along His narrow lane.
I'll never walk the path alone;
At my side, He'll always stay.
So, when the trials of life arrive
And I'm on the valley floor,
I think of how He's faithful been
And will be forevermore.
The memories of the mountaintop,
When I leapt upon the heights,
Will keep me strong on valley floor
For I'm availed of God's own might.
For my strength is in the Sovereign LORD,
There's no other with such might.
He helps me stand, sure like the deer,
Who leap upon the heights.

MY WEAPONS

I only have two weapons now
To thwart the temptor's snares.
The first one is the Word of God
And the second one is prayer.
And all who do not have these tools,
Who don't know Christ as Lord,
Will fail to see what power is mine
Contained in God's own Word.

I stand upon the promises
I read in each dear line.
I know that they will never fail
For their power is divine.
The temptor does not like it when
I kneel and call Christ's name
Because he knows the power within
And knows the power I claim.

He does not like to see me read
The words that God ordained
For in God's word it clearly states
He'll suffer hell's hot flames.
No matter what the circumstance
I use the Word and prayer
And rest secure from Satan's traps
As I rest within God's care.

OBEY MY COMMANDMENTS

These commandments that I give you today are to be
upon your hearts. Impress them on your children. Talk
about them when you sit at home and when you walk
along the road, when you lie down and when you get up.

Deuteronomy 6: 6-7 NIV

You must bear all my commandments
Down deep within your hearts.
And never from these precepts
Allow yourself to part.
Impress them on your children
And don't let them forget
All of my love and faithfulness-
All needs, some wishes met.
You must always talk about them
When you walk along the road,
When you lie and when you rise up,
To the young and to the old.
For when my laws are heeded,
My rich blessings will abound,
And my peace and joy and mercy
In your life will e'er be found.

POEM OF THANKS

My heart was heavy-laden
As I walked up to your throne.
I thought you would reject me
For I knew what I had done.

I spoke the words so softly
In humility and shame.
I told you of my sin, Lord,
And then you called my name.

**"My child, my dear precious child,
Do not let your heart be sore.
Fore'er now I forgive you.
You need be sad no more."**

My heart soared with those words, Lord,
My spirit reached heights above.
My shame and sadness fled, Lord,
With those wondrous words of love.

REFINED AND REJOICING

But he knows the way that I take; when he has tested me,
I will come forth as gold. My feet have closely followed
his steps; I have kept to his way without turning aside.

Job 23:10-11 NIV

The Master stokes the fires hot
And on the flames my life is tossed.
The dross is gone, the gold set free
Great is the prize and great the cost.
For when I rise from off the flames
My life holds nothing but the good.
The suffering that was there endured
Will shape me as I know it should.
Why question all the flames and fire
When I reside in God's own plan?
Instead, rejoicing fills my heart.
Only believers understand
That when we rest in God's great will
His plan is always for our best.
Refining will involve some pain
But gold will stay at end of test.
So, Father, search my heart and know
If there be any sin in me,
And if it's found, then light the fire
And set my golden spirit free.
Unshackled by sin's blackened dross,
I'll soar beneath your watchful eye,
And come to rest on heaven's shore
In that great land of by-and-by.

REJOICE AND WEEP

*"Rejoice with them that do rejoice, and
weep with them that weep."*

Romans 12:15 KJV

Rejoice with them that do rejoice,
And weep with them that weep.
In doing this each day you live,
God's law of love you'll keep.
It matters not if foe or friend.
God's love should be the mark
That we choose for our actions,
Which must be rooted in our hearts.
We should not wait and justify
If we will love or not.
God's word should be our mandate
In our actions, words and thoughts.
So weep with those who know a loss;
Let God's love, through you, shine.
Rejoice with those who do rejoice
And obey God's law divine.

RISE UP, O LAMB

Rise up, My Little Lamb, and stand
For we have far to go.
Our shepherds roused us from our sleep
Due to all that they've been shown.
I heard them tell of angel choirs
Who sang that a king was born.
They'd find him in small Bethlehem,
In a manger all forlorn.
But, Momma, I'm still tired
And I want to go to sleep.
The night is cold around me
And the darkness is so deep.
My Little Lamb, please stay awake
For the shepherds said we must;
The shepherds know what's best for us
So in their wisdom we must trust.
They go to seek that newborn king
In Bethlehem's small town.
So rise up now, My Little Lamb.
Please don't grumble. Please don't frown.
Okay, dear Momma, I will go
As you have asked me to.
You put your trust in the shepherd's care
And I put my trust in you.

My legs are tired. Can't we stop
And rest here for a while?
No, Lamb of Mine, we must move on
And walk these extra miles.

Momma, Momma, do you see that star
That's shining in the night?
It's stopping over that stable there
With a truly glorious light.

Yes, Lamb, I see that glowing star.
Our journey's end is near.
I heard the shepherds talk about
The angels' message clear.
The angels said the world's King
Was born to bring men peace,
And to fill repentant hearts that call
With a love that will not cease.

**Momma, can we get up close
And see this newborn King
Whose birth the shepherds heard about
When they heard the angels sing?**
Yes, Lamb of Mine, walk up and see
The world's King on the hay.
It's a truly wonderful time for you
For you'll see your Creator today.
**But, Momma, he's so little.
The king's just a baby boy.**
Yes, Lamb, but when he's all grown up,
The world will try destroy
The truth that he will teach them,
Of salvation, pain and loss.
That little baby will grow up
And die upon the cross.
The blood that will flow freely there
On Calvary's cruel hill
Will save all mankind from his sin,
And prophecy fulfill.
**Oh, Momma, I'm so sad now
That this little one will die,
That sinful hearts will never know
That he came from up on high.**

Rejoice, My Lamb, because that King
Will die, but rise again;
That resurrection will ensure
That man's heart might have no stain.
He knew God's great redemption plan;
He knew it from the start.
And yet He yielded up his life
To cleanse man's sin-stained heart.
Oh, Momma, what can I do now
To thank him, if I can?
Oh, Lamb of Mine, just yield your heart
And remember Christ, the Lamb.

SEEKER AND SAVIOR

*"For the Son of Man came to seek
and to save what was lost."*

Luke 19:10 NIV

The Son of Man left from glory
To seek and save the lost.
He knew his Father's saving plan,
Yet never let the cost
Of sacrifice and gruesome death
Deter him from God's plan;
He knew it was the only way
To redeem fallen man.
He sought me in sin's darkness
And brought me to the light.
And throughout all my earthly days,
I'll see his power and might.
I know that my soul would be lost,
And headed straight for hell
But by God's mercy, grace and love,
A new story I now tell.
With Jesus Christ as centre,
With Jesus as my King,
I know that in his love and grace,
He'll grant me everything –
Not as the world sees it,
But he'll provide my needs
And he will never leave me,
As I praise in word and deeds.
And my heart's desire is to remain
And in his love abide
Until my time in glory,
When I'll walk by his side.
I'll praise him as my Seeker,
Who sought me in my sin
And praise him as my Savior,
Who cleansed me deep within.

SOWING AND REAPING

Do not be deceived: God cannot be mocked. A man reaps what he sows. The one who sows to please his sinful nature, from that nature will reap destruction; the one who sows to please the Spirit, from the Spirit will reap eternal life.

Galatians 6:7-8 NIV

Please, Brother, do not be deceived;
Our God cannot be mocked.
Each thought is heard and each deed seen;
His vision like a hawk.
The night can't hide the deeds we do
That go against His word,
For everything's open to His sight.
He is the sovereign Lord.
Whatever a man or woman sows
Will be just what they reap.
So good must be the seed you sow
As you, God's decrees, keep.
Sowing to please the nature of sin
Will reap destruction true.
But sowing to please the Spirit
Will reap eternal life for you.
So, Brother, listen to God's words
For it means a lot to know
That life's harvest is dependent on
The good or bad we sowed.

STEPS OF LOVE

You placed one foot in front of
The one you placed before.
You stumbled and fell under
The heavy load you bore.

You never once considered
To call your angels near.
You kept my sin in mind, Lord,
As you heard the crowd's loud jeers.

They cursed your name, dear Jesus.
You focused on the goal.
Your sacrifice was needed
To cleanse and make me whole.

And though it still amazes
That a king would leave above,
I'll be forever grateful
That you took those steps of love.

SUCCESS AND FAILURE

Does success only mean that your bank account's full,
That there's plenty to buy what you see?
Or is failure defined as not having enough
To supply all the things you may need?

Is success just a measure of the things you've acquired,
All the things that will rot and decay?
Or is failure a measure of just what you don't have,
All the good things that the world says is okay?

The world's definition of success is all wrong,
And a failure is defined wrongly as well.
But, just listen and hear what the right meaning is
As from my vantage point I will tell.

Success lies in knowing that you're loved by the Lord,
That His love for you will never end,
That His grace, love and mercy that He daily will show
Will be your strength as, on Him, you depend.

Success will be knowing that great peace from God
As you pillow your head down each night,
And the joy and contentment will be gifts from above
As you rest within God's holy sight.

Now I define failure as not heeding the Word
And not yielding your life to God's care,
And you will not experience the great blessings bestowed
On those who daily Christ's precious cross bear.

So now, in your own mind, you must choose how the terms
"To succeed' and "to fail" are defined.
And I pray that your choice will lead right to Christ
And His grace and His love you will find.

THANK YOU, LORD

I come to you with empty hands,
And with a humble heart I stand.
For nothing, Lord, that I now own
Could repay you for what you've done.

You cleansed my soul and set me free,
Your love displayed on Calv'ry's tree.
You paid the price for my dark debt –
That great a price I won't forget.

And, with the time I have on Earth,
I'll spend it all to tell your worth
To others who have not been told.
(Please help me, Lord, to be so bold).

So they will know of your great love
And give their lives to You, above.
I'll join them all in songs of praise
When you complete my earthly days.

"THANK YOU" IS NOT QUITE ENOUGH

"Thank you" does not seem quite enough
For all that you have done.
You've given me salvation
Through Jesus Christ, your Son.

I've been shown love from you, my God,
From friends and family too.
All that I hold most dear in life
Were all bestowed by you.

There's not a minute in a day
I'm not led by your hand;
Your promise to not leave, forsake,
I know and understand.

There's food upon my table
And a roof over my head.
My heart securely rests each night
As I'm sleeping in my bed.

You give me peace that knows no bounds;
Your grace is multiplied.
Your mercy's great, I can attest,
When I am being tried.

But, if I had to rank the things
That, in love for me, you've done,
The first thing on my thankful list
Would be Jesus Christ, your Son.

For, with His death on Calvary,
His love for me was plain.
A sin-stained heart, turned white as snow,
Will never be the same.

But His death alone did not ensure
That in that judgment hour,
My soul would find a home in heaven;
It was His resurrection hour.

When, in great might, He rose again
And now sits at your right hand
To advocate for His chosen ones,
In near and foreign lands.

So, I will try to live your will,
Though the going may get tough
For that's the least I can do for you,
For thank you is not enough.

THAT HAND

The hand that moved over the vast expanse
And caused land and water to part-
That hand is all sufficient for me
For the power it can still impart.

The hand that wrote on the tablets of stone
All the statutes, laws and decrees-
That hand is all sufficient for me
For it's all that I really need.

The hand that told the Red Sea to part
And stand like a wall on both sides-
That hand is all sufficient for me
For I need no other thing besides.

The hand that holds the sceptre of righteousness
And writes in the Book of Life-
That hand is all sufficient for me
No matter what trouble is rife.

And no matter what situation I'm in
I hope that you will understand
That my God will save all who call on His name
For we're held in the palm of that hand.

THE CHOICE OF A LIFETIME

How much better to get wisdom than gold, to
choose understanding rather than silver!

Proverbs 16:16 NIV

A treasure has value in the mind of the man
Whose goal is to gather as much as he can.
His values determine which one he will choose
When given a choice, will he win? Will he lose?

One man will choose gold as the thing he loves most.
His wealth and possessions, of this he will boast.
There's no satisfying his lust for the goal;
It stays with him always 'til the death bells would toll.

Or maybe it is silver that drives man to crave,
To hoard and to covet that gleam to the grave.
He knows not that something that's gained on this earth
Will ne'er enter heaven, for it won't hold its worth.

But the man who will quest after wisdom always
Will see how God prospers him throughout his days.
And true understanding will be his reward
As his steps take him closer each day to the Lord.

So think on this matter, and which you would choose
If the choices were given. Would you win? Would you lose?
Would wisdom lose out to the glint of the gold
Or silver be chosen over the insights of old?

For wherever your mind puts the value most dear,
Your choices reflect that in ways that are clear.
Will you gather the silver and gold of this earth,
Or give wisdom and understanding their worth?

THE FIRST CHRISTMAS GIFTS

I looked at the tree
With its lights all aglow,
And presents beneath it
All tied with a bow.
Not just one gift per person,
But many for all.
Over this great abundance,
The green tree stood tall.
And I gazed at the picture
In my living room there
Of the tree, oh so pretty,
All arranged with great care.
I then thought of the first tree
Of time long ago
Where a gift there was offered
God's great love to show.
There was nothing pretty
About Calvary's tree,
Just a rough-hewn old cross
Where my Lord's blood ran free.
And Christ's cruel death means
My heart bears no stain
For the grave could not hold him
And he's living again.
That gift that was given
Which was prophecy fulfilled
Had begun back in Bethlehem,
A little town on a hill.
The choirs of angels
Led men from afar
To the stable ablaze
With the light of a star.
The shepherds bowed low
When they came to my King,
And rejoiced in the news
They had heard angels sing

That a king had been born
Who would save fallen man,
All according to God's great
And glorious plan.
And the wise men presented
Their rich gifts of gold,
And myrrh and some frankincense,
As the story's been told.
Christ's birth in that stable
Was God's first gift to me,
And his death on the cross
Was the second, you see.
For the cross could not happen
Unless Christ came to earth,
And willingly relinquished
All heaven's great worth,
And took on the form
Of frail dust-made man,
In order to accomplish
God's salvation plan.
So he yielded his life
On dark Calvary's tree
For all hearts of repentance,
For you and for me.
God's gifts had no wrapping,
No bows tied them neat.
No ribbon or sparkles
To make them complete,
But their value can never
Be given a price.
It's a love gift from God,
When he gifted us twice.

THE FOOL

The fool says in his heart, "There is no God." They are corrupt, their deeds are vile; there is no one who does good.

Psalm 14:1 NIV

The one who says there is no God
Is a fool beyond degree.
For God's creation cries His name
For all who choose to see.
The mountains stand in majesty;
The flowers and trees are there.
The birds and beasts of all the earth
Are held in the Master's care.
The fool draws breath and does not see
That God himself sustains.
The wonder of man's human form
God's mighty power proclaims.
His thinking's wrong and so corrupt;
His deeds are dark and vile.
He thinks he holds the power in life
And God's own power reviles.
And yet, one day, that fool will bow
And acknowledge God's true power.
When repentance fills his contrite heart
Or at the judgment hour.
So, Friend, believe that God is here
With omnipotent power and grace
And yield your heart to Him in love;
He'll help you win life's race.
And when the time of death draws near
And the course is almost done,
Then look ahead to the finish line
And see the Father and the Son.

THE GATES AND THE ROADS

*Enter through the narrow gate. For wide is the gate
and broad is the road that leads to destruction, and
many enter through it. But small is the gate and narrow
the road that leads to life, and only a few find it.*

Matthew 7:13-14 NIV

The road that leads to destruction
Is broad and is very well-trod.
But narrow the road bound for heaven
That arrives at the home of God.
The gate that leads to destruction
Is grand and remains open wide.
This gate does not bar any entry
And many will enter inside.
The gate that will gain one the access
To heaven and all that it holds,
Is small and not many enter –
Just the sheep of the Master's fold.
Choose now the road you will follow,
Choose which gate you'll open up wide.
One leads to hell and damnation;
One leads straight to the Redeemer's side.

THE LORD IS WATCHING

*The LORD will keep you from all harm – he will
watch over your life; the LORD will watch over your
coming and going both now and forevermore."*

Psalm 121:7-8 NIV

The good LORD will keep you from any harm;
His watchfulness will never end.
Your coming and going is overseen.
On this fact you can depend.

There's not been a time when He wasn't there
From the moment that time began.
His love and His mercy, His extended grace
Are all part of God's master plan.

He'll be right beside you in days to come;
You never will walk alone.
His word says he'll never leave nor forsake,
To the time when He'll call you home.

And then, up in glory, you'll rest in His care
And praise Him for life fresh and new
And, with grateful heart, you'll bow 'fore His throne
And thank Him for caring for you.

THE POWER OF GOD'S LOVE

For I am convinced that neither death nor life, neither
angels nor demons, neither the present nor the future,
nor any powers, neither height nor depth, nor anything
else in all creation, will be able to separate us from
the love of God that is in Christ Jesus our Lord.

Romans 8:38-39 NIV

Angels and demons do not have the power
To sever the strong bonds of love
That we receive from our Lord, Jesus Christ
And our Father in heaven above.

Death cannot do it; Christ defeated the grave.
No power on earth can they claim.
When trials and temptations come and surround,
We just need to call on His name.

Neither height nor depth, or creation itself
Can break the great love that God shows.
His love is eternal, compassionate, too.
Each believer, in faith, this fact knows.

So, Satan and minions, just listen and learn
I believe that your power is crushed.
For when I rest within the love of my God
I remain much-loved, at peace, and untouched.

THE SHEEP KNOW THE SHEPHERD

My sheep listen to my voice; I know them, and they follow me. I give them eternal life, and they shall never perish; no one will snatch them out of my hand. My Father, who has given them to me, is greater than all; no one can snatch them out of my Father's hand. I and the Father are one."

John 10:27-30 NIV

My sheep listen to my voice;
They know and follow me.
Eternal life I give to them;
No spiritual death they'll see.
No one can snatch them from my hand;
They rest in me secure.
They rest within my Father's hand,
And their safety there is sure.
For my Father gave them to me,
And my Father is greater than all.
My sheep don't fret or worry
For all they need do is call.
These words you spoke, dear Jesus,
About security and care.
I, too, am a sheep within your flock
And know love without compare.
So, Lord, help me to listen
To your whispers and your shouts,
And in my quiet obedience
There'll be no room for doubts.
I thank you for your Shepherd's care,
Your presence in my life.
You're my heavenly protector
In the midst of woe and strife.

THE TRUTH OF THE CROSS

For the message of the cross is foolishness to those who are perishing, but to us who are being saved it is the power of God."

1 Corinthians 1:18 NIV

For those who do not know Jesus Christ,
The Cross is foolishness.
They have not realized the fact
They must their sins confess.
Their fate is sealed with their decision
To reject Christ, the King,
And naught, except repentance true,
Will change a single thing.
But those that have the knowledge
Of the greatness of their sin
Will fall down on their knees and ask
The blessed Savior in.
Those who call on Jesus' name
Will have their sins forgiven
And have within a quiet faith
That their final home is heaven.
They will confess all of their sins
In that true life-changing hour
And find God's mercy, grace and love,
And his amazing power;
A power that ever can transcend
All distance, time and space
Will be his gift to those who call
And encounter his great grace.
It's only by the death of Christ
That dark day on Calvary
We're guaranteed eternal life
And given the victory.

For without that act of selfless love,
Our fates would be sealed too,
And we would all be bound for hell,
Without a thing to do.
But God, in his salvation plan,
Sent Christ to earth to be
A sacrificial lamb who died
For all people, you and me.
But death could not contain him
And he arose in power and might
And rose to sit at God's right hand,
A place that is his right.
He intercedes with God for us,
An advocate so true,
And all who call on Jesus' name,
Will gain a life renewed.

THERE IS NONE LIKE YOU

LORD, there is no one like you to help the powerless against the mighty. Help us, LORD our God, for we rely on you, and in your name we have come against this vast army. LORD, you are our God; do not let mere mortals prevail against you.

2 Chronicles 14:11

Lord, there is no one that's like you.
You uphold the cause of the weak,
If they will just bow down to serve you,
And your face, every hour, they do seek.

The dark Temptor's army surrounds us;
In our strength we will never prevail.
But we know, that with our God on our side,
In the battle with Satan, we won't fail.

You alone, Lord Jesus, are our God;
Our hearts now to you, Lord, belong.
And we pray that the army against us
Can see your might, so great and so strong.

THIS EARTH IS NOT MY HOME

I am a wanderer on this earth;
My home is far away.
My home is far above the clouds,
Beyond both time or days.

I was put here to praise my Lord
For all that He has done
And, as I pass along the way,
I'll talk of God's own son.

I'll tell each one of sacrifice,
A cross, and blood and pain.
I'll tell of God's redemption plan
To atone for man's sin stain.

And I will tell of His great love
And His amazing power
That wrested victory from the grave
In His resurrection hour.

When I no longer walk this earth,
My journey here all done,
I'll soar up to my heavenly home
And be welcomed by God's son.

THROUGH

You got your people through the sea
When Pharoah chased them down.
And when they'd walked through on dry land,
Then Pharoah's army drowned.
You got Daniel through the lion's den,
He never got a scratch.
His faith was what had saved him, Lord;
He knew you had no match.

You got Shadrach and Abednego,
And Meshach through the flames.
Your hand was on their lives, Lord,
For they called upon your name.
You helped David gain the victory
When the giant should have won.
His faith in you was unsurpassed
And Goliath's end was done.

I know that you can get me through
Whatever comes my way.
You did it for men long ago,
And your power's the same today.
So, Lord, help me to not despair
When trouble rears its head.
I know that you are with me;
By your loving hand I'm led.

UNIMAGINABLE

*However, as it is written: What no eye has seen, what no
ear has heard, and what no human mind has conceived...
the things God has prepared for those who love him*

1 Corinthians 2:9 NIV

The human mind will never grasp
The reward that lies in store.
Our wildest dreams are but a mote,
For the Lord will give us more.
Our eyes have never seen on earth
What waits us far beyond,
And sounds unheard by human ears
In heaven will be found.
The sight of jasper walls and such,
And streets made out of gold -
Our feeble mind can't comprehend
All that we have been told.
And sights we deem as beautiful,
In heaven won't compare
With all the light and colours
That believers will find there.
The sound of praise will fill the air,
Combined with angel voice,
As saints of all the ages past
Will stand and will rejoice
For all that Christ has done for them,
Of lives that were renewed.
The sound will fill our hearts so full
We won't know what to do.
And while I walk down here on earth
In my time that God ordained,
I'll tell the lost how Christ had died
To cleanse man's dark soul stain.
But when my soul slips from this earth,
And I walk this earth no more,
I'll know the true reality
Of what God has set in store.

WALKING IN THE DESERT

I'm walking in the desert, Lord.
My soul is parched and dry.
I do not know if I can last,
So on your name I'll cry.

You've been with me on valley floor,
And you have seen me through
The times of deep despair and woe.
My life I owe to you!

I know that you've shown faithfulness
To me throughout the years.
You've held my hand so I won't fall
And dried up all my tears.

So now I know that I will be
Secure within your arms.
I'll walk upright and look ahead
With no fear and no alarms.

You've said that you will never leave;
You never will forsake.
I'll stand upon the promises
That in your Word you state.

So, next time I'm in desert place,
Help me, Lord, to recall
Your might, your mercy and your grace.
You are my all-in-all.

WHAT A VISION

For the Lord himself shall descend from heaven with a shout, with the voice of the archangel, and with the trump of God: and the dead in Christ shall rise first: Then we which are alive and remain shall be caught up together with them in the clouds, to meet the Lord in the air: and so shall we ever be with the Lord.

1 Thessalonians 4:16-17 KJV

The Lord himself will descend from heaven;
He will come with a shout we can hear.
The archangel's voice will be heard at that time,
And the dead in Christ will appear.

They will have risen from their graves,
From their beds of no worry or care.
Then, we who are still alive and remain,
Will be caught up with them in the air.

There we will meet the Lord, our true King,
And what joy will then fill our souls,
Just to know that for all of eternity,
From His presence we never will go.

What a vision these words put on my heart,
And with hope I can anticipate,
The joy that I'll know when the Lord's face I see,
Though I know not the time or the date.

Yet, I know that these words have great import;
They're infallible, inerrant and true.
They contain God's great plan that will happen;
They tell us what the Lord God will do.

So, prepare for the time of Christ's coming,
Though you know not the time or the place.
Call on His name now for forgiveness;
To a repentant heart, He'll give grace.

WHAT DID YOU DO WITH MY SON?

When I stand 'fore His throne up in glory,
When my race here on earth is all run,
God will ask me one single question,
"Tell me, what did you do with my Son?
What did you do with His bounteous grace
Bestowed in your time of great trial?
What did you do with His great sacrifice,
When He hung there being reviled?
What did you do with the fact that He took
The punishment owed by your sins?
How did you feel when you called on His name
And had soul cleansed so deeply within?
How busy were you in spreading the news
To the lost on the byways of life?
Did you tell them, each chance, of the peace availed
In the midst of life's struggles and strife?
I pray when God questions, I'll be able to say,
"I accepted your Son as my Lord.
I took opportunity to spread the Good News,
As it commands in your Holy Word."
I hope that there's someone who's gone on before
Who can say, "The reason I'm here
Is because this good person had chosen to share
My need for salvation, so clear."
'Til then I will labour, for Christ, every day
And I'll tell all the lost that I meet
Of God's love and mercy, His grace and His peace,
And, like Christ, I will try meet their need.

WHAT LIES AHEAD

I've started on the path ahead.
I know not where it ends.
Will each step be in weather fair
Or blustery round each bend?
The path, will it remain so smooth
That I can walk in peace,
Or will it change to ruts and grooves
That do not seem to cease?
I cannot know what lies ahead
As I take steps each hour.
I know the Lord walks with me,
And I'm availed of His great power.
I know that as we walk along
On the smooth or rugged road,
He'll be right there to lend a hand
When I can't bear the load.
I know that I'm held firmly
In the palm of Jesus' hand.
He'll never let me go from Him;
His love I know and understand.
And when Satan sets snares in my path,
I will stumble but won't fall,
For I will hold the hand of Christ.
He is my all in all.
I'll never see the path's end point,
As I take steps each day.
I'll keep my eyes fixed on the Lord.
He's the Truth, the Life, the Way.
I'll look beyond the daily path,
And to my earthly end,
When that last step is taken
And glory's round the bend.
And as I look back on the path
When earthly time is gone,
I pray that Christ will smile and say,
"Well done, my child, well done."

WHAT YOU DID FOR ME

Your strength's revealed when I am weak,
And, in those times, your face I seek.
I know that you are always near,
To hold my hand or dry a tear.
No power on earth can e'er prevail
For your great power will never fail.
And Satan cannot ever win
For you have saved me from my sin.
You cleansed a heart destined for hell.
You made me yours, complete and well.
No longer do I have to fear
For you'll always be standing near.
So, Jesus, may I always be
Found in your strength for all to see.
May I each day be bold to tell
How your great love saved me from hell.
I'll always thank you for your grace,
For hanging tortured in my place.
May I relinquish all I am
To you, God's sacrificial Lamb.

WHEN I WALK BESIDE MY SAVIOR

When I walk beside my Savior,
The world has lost its power
Due to Christ's death on Calvary
And His resurrection hour.

No king or principality,
No man, no throne can harm.
When I walk beside my Savior
I am held within His arms.

The world can never satisfy
The longing in my heart
For peace and joy and comfort
Christ's loving kindness does impart.

And when the world announces
That god rests in man within,
It's not the God of heaven
Whose plan atoned man's sin.

For all who have repentant hearts
Will come to Calvary
And there receive a life brand new
And Christ's love and grace will see.

A love that covers all the shame
And guilt from man's dark past.
A love that will not ever forsake.
A love that will always last.

His love is mine throughout my days,
And in Him I will abide,
And abundant life, in Christ, is mine
As my Savior I walk beside.

WHEN WE WORK FOR THE LORD

*God is not unjust; he will not forget your work
and the love you have shown him as you have
helped his people and continue to help them.*

Hebrews 6:10 NIV

When we work daily for the Lord
As it's ordained in His own Word,
He will never forget our deeds
And His great blessing we'll receive.
All His love that we have shown
Unto His people we have known
Will be rewarded, His word says,
In all His holy, wondrous ways.
While here on earth, his love and grace
Will multiply in every case,
As those in need have needs well met
In ways that they'll not soon forget.
Because our God is not unjust,
In His great love each one must trust,
And know that every deed we do
Is seen by God, remembered too.
A robe, a mansion up in heaven
Will be rewards that we'll be given.
A crown and robe of righteousness
Will be ours too, and nothing less.
For God, who sees all acts of love
Will say, "Well done" when we soar above.

WHO CAN COMPARE
TO THE GLORY OF GOD?

For all have sinned and fall short of the glory of God, and are justified freely by his grace through the redemption that came by Christ Jesus.

Romans 3:23-24 NIV

Fallen man, though he try hard,
Cannot compare with the glory of God.
For all have sinned and won't come near
To the glory of God. Let all who hear
Exalt his name, and give him praise
For the working of his marvelous grace.
His grace bestowed, to us no cost,
But it meant His son died on the cross.
He died a death, so grave to see,
But it ensured my victory.
When through his rising that third day
He offered man redemption's way
To save all people broken-hearted
And have God's grace, so rich, imparted.
And those who bring repentant hearts
Will find a love that won't depart.
We are assured that we will spend
Eternity with God, and without end,
We'll sing and praise him for his grace
Throughout our lives and then face-to-face.

WHO IS GOD?

One day a man sat 'neath a tree
And wondered in his mind –
If I asked people "Who is God?",
I wonder what I'd find.

A worm came wiggling on the ground
And looked up at the man.
"The world you see around you, Sir,
Is part of God's great plan.
There's nothing that you'll see, my friend,
That God did not create.
The big, the small, the in-between.
My God is really great!"

And then a bird flew down and said,
"My God is truly grand.
I never have to be concerned,
For I rest in His hand.
I do not worry what to eat,
For God will care for me.
Each day I get my food supply,
Some seeds and forest tree.

A dog came barking to the man,
And stopped when he was asked,
"I know that God can do it all,
Both large and smaller tasks.
There is no problem He can't solve,
No circumstance that stops
His might and power from being revealed.
My God is just the tops!"

A large black cat was next to speak,
"My God's a God of love.
He watches over those He loves
From heaven up above.

He'll always send His mercy
When trouble shows its face,
And to those folks who wear his name,
He always shows His grace."

The man was quite confused now,
The answer wasn't there.
He didn't have the answer
Though all the others shared.
He wondered if he'd ever really
Know the facts for sure,
And wondered if his questions
Would for all time endure.

But then another man came by,
And made the first man glad.
With just a few words, it was clear
The answers this man had.
"I know that God takes care of those
Who walk His narrow way.
He loves His people and provides
All that they need each day.

He is a God of power and might,
Of mercy and of grace,
He is a God of faithfulness.
Don't put any in His place.
He is a God who will forgive
All that we've said and done.
He is a God who wants to welcome us
To heaven, our real home.

The man still sat beneath his tree,
But now he knew the truth.
"My God is all the things you said,
And my God loves you too."

WHY NOT?

When you show me what you will for me,
I sometimes stand in fear
For I know all the things that I cannot do,
But your voice is true and clear.

I know that you'll walk with me each day.
I know you'll never leave.
I know that, only by your mercy and grace,
The victory I'll receive.

So now I'll replace my fear and doubt;
I'll think a brand new thought.
Instead of saying "Who, me, Lord?"
I'll answer "Lord, why not?"

WITH GOD ON YOUR SIDE

Be brave and courageous.
Stand firm in the fight.
You're under protection
Of God's power and might.
No kingdom or power
Will ever prevail.
Keep holding to God's hand,
And you will not fail.
Remember what God's done
Each time in the past.
Remember that His grace
And mercy will last.
His love will surround you
In trials or tests;
Do not become anxious;
And do not become stressed.
Remember God's close by
And think this thought true,
That if you stand beside God
Who can stand against you?

WONDERING QUESTIONS

What do I have
If I have not your favour?
What would I have
If Christ counted the cost?
Where would my soul dwell
When death tolls were ringing?
I know that, in all these,
My soul would be lost.

Why should I praise you
For what you have done, God?
Why should I think on
Your faithfulness, Lord?
Why have communion
With Christ, my Redeemer?
I know it's a mandate
Of your Holy Word.

Why should I tell
The lost ones of your great love?
Why should I tell them
Christ's grace set them free?
Why should I try
To build bridges between us?
It is because
Of what Christ did for me.

How would they know
About Calvary and Jesus?
How could they know
That He rose from the grave?
How could they ever
Yield their life up to Him
If I did not tell them
That Christ is the Way?

When is the time
That is perfect to tell them?
What circumstances
Must be met so I'm heard?
What if I'm not
In the right space or moment?
I will not worry
For I'll be led by the Lord.

WORTHY WARDROBE

Wear compassion as a mantle
And a cloak of kindness cloth.
So others see that you're chosen
And dearly loved by the Lord.
Wear humility on your back
Gentleness and patience too,
And all good things that come from God
Will be given unto you.
But do it not for that reward,
Just do it for the Lord.
Apply the lessons you have learned
As you read within His word.
For those that hate their brother
And wish to cause him pain,
Will reap the wrath of God himself
And death will be their gain.
A death that sees no ending
In the fiery flames of hell.
So, listen and obey God
And your life will turn out well.
Compassion, kindness, patience
Gentleness and humility
Should be the wardrobe that you wear
To gain the crown of victory.

YOU

You left a holy crown of glory
And wore a crown of thorns.
You came to earth, full God, full man,
On that blessed Christmas morn.

You came not as a conqueror
With armies at your call.
You came instead as redeeming King
To be my all in all.

You walked this earth in human form
And preached to sinful man
That all with a repentant heart
Will be ransomed by God's plan.

And though you knew that sacrifice
Upon dark Calvary's tree
Was needed to redeem my soul,
You showed your love for me.

You walked those steps of love that day;
You bore that cruel cross,
Because you knew you'd have to die
So my soul would not be lost.

You hung upon that cross in pain
And asked your father to forgive
The ones below that taunted you.
Your example may I live!

"It is done!" you whispered in your pain
And then your voice was stilled.
But after three days in the tomb
You arose and God's plan fulfilled.

My soul is free, and my life brand new.
I know I'll never see
Why you could have spared yourself that pain,
But your thoughts were all of me.

You loved me so much that you chose
To ransom my dark soul,
To clean my life from deep within
And make my spirit whole.

So with a humble grateful heart,
I speak these words so true,
"I'll ever praise you for your grace.
All that I need is you."

YOU ARE GOD

Before the mountains were born or you brought forth the earth and the world, from everlasting to everlasting you are God. For a thousand years in your sight are like a day that has just gone by, or like a watch in the night.

Psalm 90:2,4 NIV

You are God
Before the mountains rose over the earth.
You are God
Before you had ever brought forth the world.
You are God
Before time was established by mortal man.
You are God
Before you created your salvation plan.
You are God
Before Eden's Garden and Adam and Eve.
You are God
Before the first soul had ever believed.
You are God
Before whose throne each person will come.
You are God
Before whom the saints are all welcomed home.
You are God
Before judgment points to heaven or hell.
You are God
Before whom we'll hear, "My child, you've done well."

Before man was created and on this earth trod,
In the past, present and future, you are God.

YOU HAVE BEEN GOOD TO ME

LORD, you have assigned me my portion and my cup;
you have made my lot secure. You have made known
to me the path of life; you will fill me with joy in your
presence, with eternal pleasures at your right hand.

Psalm 16: 5, 11 NIV

You've assigned me my portion
And assigned me my cup.
When the world makes me stumble,
You help me stand up.
Secure is my lot, Lord,
For you have made known
The pathway of life, Lord,
And your great love you've shown.
I rejoice in your presence,
For what more could I ask
Than the eternal pleasures
From your righteous right hand?
When this earth I no longer
Walk with human constraints,
Your praise will be the anthem
That I sing with the saints.
And I know that forever,
I will sing that sweet song,
That my sins were forgiven
And to Christ I belong.

YOUR CREATION

The mountains with their mighty peaks
That reach up to the sky,
The worm that crawls along the earth,
And all the birds that fly,
The fish that swims within the sea,
The giraffe standing tall.
You, my God, and you alone
Have made them one and all.

The lion with its regal mane,
The smallest gnat and flea,
The snake that slithers in the grass,
The whales within the sea,
The elephant with size and might,
All that on this earth trod,
Without a doubt, I know it's true
They were made by you, my God.

But nature was not all you made,
For you created humans, too.
Man was your creation, God,
To bring glory unto you.
But man's great sin defiled your plan,
And yet you showed him love.
You sent your son to die for him
Your amazing grace to prove.

I thank you for creation, God,
That all around I see.
And through Christ's death on Calvary,
My soul knows liberty.
What joy I do anticipate
When my soul slips this flawed earth,
And I meet my Savior face-to-face.
I will praise for all I'm worth!

YOUR HANDS

Your hands have all this world made –
Majestic mountain, grassy blade,
Each bird with sound unique and sweet,
Each child within the womb complete,
Each flower garbed in colour bright,
Each star displayed in darkest night.

Your hands have all this world formed –
The centipede and long earthworm,
The cattle and the birds that fly
And soar up yonder in your sky,
The things that crawl upon the ground,
And those, in burrows, that are found.

Your hands held up the fish and bread
And then five thousand folk were fed.
A touch from you made a leper clean
And many miracles were seen
Of sight restored and health renewed
With nothing but a touch from you.

Your hands have made the world for me,
And, Lord, I pray you help me see
All that you've done and e'er will do,
All with a loving touch from you.
And help me grasp and understand
That I rest secure within your hands.

YOUR LOVE AND CARE, LORD

I am your creation, Lord,
A life that was reborn
When you arose in power, Lord,
That blessed Easter morn.

You alone, my Lord, control
The very breath I take.
I cannot stand without you-
Not even one step make.

The power of your love, Lord,
Allows my soul to soar
Against wind currents of distress
When I hurt to the core.

Your love will never leave me.
Your Word says this is true.
And I have all I need, Lord,
When all I have is you.

I know I sit within your hand,
And I rest in your care.
What more would I desire
Than to just stay still right there?

There is no throne or kingdom
Or power I need fear
For I rest in your love, Lord.
I know you're always near.

I know your love is constant,
And no conditions do you set
That would deny salvation
If such conditions were not met.

I only had to bring my life
With all sins from the past
And trade it for abundant life,
A life I know that'll last.

I know that time will come, Lord,
When I won't walk this earth
But, up in heaven with you, Lord,
My life will find its worth.

And throughout all the ages,
I'll worship you and praise
Your mighty power and mercy
That saved me by your grace.

YOUR TREASURE

Do not be afraid, little flock, for your Father has been pleased to give you the kingdom. Sell your possessions and give to the poor. Provide purses for yourselves that will not wear out, a treasure in heaven that will not be exhausted, where no thief comes near and no moth destroys. For where your treasure is, there your heart will be also.

Luke 12:32-34 NIV

Your Father's kingdom has been given to you,
So here are the actions believers must do.
Sell your possessions and give to the poor
A treasure in heaven this act will ensure.
A treasure that no one will ever exhaust
Nor find that, at some time, the treasure is lost.
A treasure believers can truly enjoy
Where no thief comes near and no moth destroys.
For wherever your treasure in life can be found
Your heart, and its loyalty, will also be bound.
So pick now, this day, where your treasure will be-
On earth now or heaven for eternity,
Your Father's bright hope or the world's loud acclaim,
God's richest blessings or eternal shame,
Eternity shared with God and his Son
Or hell's destination when life here is done.
You must make a choice each day that you live;
I pray the right answer is the one that you give.